JOSEPH BANKS

A Life From Beginning to End

Copyright © 2018 by Hourly History.

All rights reserved.

Table of Contents

Introduction
Early Years
Civil Engineer
The Big Stink
Metropolitan Commissions for Sewers
Metropolitan Board of Works
Bazalgette's Plan
The Embankments
Transport for London
Bridges Across the Thames
Conclusion

Introduction

Sir Joseph Bazalgette was an engineer who designed and built a system of sewers and pumping stations which transformed the River Thames. By 1858, the river was, quite literally, a flowing cesspool. This was due to the huge amounts of sewage being emptied directly into the river from the homes of millions of Londoners. The outlet of sewage, in turn, had been brought about in the middle of the nineteenth century by legislation which abolished home cesspools in favor of connection to a system of sewage tunnels which emptied into the river.

Within 20 years of the invention of the water closet and the legislation requiring all toilets be connected to the sewers, the river had been stripped of all life and had become a health hazard. Sir Joseph Bazalgette changed that. As chief engineer to the Metropolitan Board of Works, he designed a system of intercepting sewers that would prevent effluent being dumped into the river anywhere but the least populated districts. His main sewer system was so effective that it virtually wiped out instances of cholera, typhus, and typhoid almost overnight in London. Bazalgette innovated in designs to ensure that his constructions stood the test of time. His main sewers survive and are effective to this day due to the skill with which they were designed.

Bazalgette also had the foresight to make use of materials such as Portland cement and Staffordshire blue bricks which other engineers wouldn't risk. He devised means of testing his materials to ensure quality, which formed the basis of minimum standards throughout the industry, and thus he improved the quality of building and engineering projects that would follow.

Bazalgette rebuilt London, building more of it than anyone had done since the aftermath of the Great Fire in 1666. Under his designs, slum dwellings deemed unfit for human habitation were demolished, and new thoroughfares sprang up which made travel from one part of the city to the other more comfortable by easing traffic congestion. His bridge designs enabled poor workers from south of the river to cross, for free, to jobs in the north.

Parks designed by him, a free ferry service, a sewer system, and a network of new roads all survive to this day. All serve the purpose for which they were designed, standing as proof of the thoroughness and skill of the man.

Chapter One

Early Years

"This superb and far-sighted engineer probably did more good, and saved more lives, than any single Victorian public official."

—*The Observer*, April 14, 1861

Joseph William Bazalgette was of French descent. His grandfather, Jean-Louis Bazalgette, was born in a small village of Ispagnac in the Massif Central region of France. The family was long-lived and amongst the nobility of the country. Ispagnac appears close to the village of La Bazalgette in the Auvergne region, but the origins of the family are lost in history. One source suggests that the name may derive from the Turkish Bajazet. Bazalgettes do appear in French history from the thirteenth century onwards, with one Raymond Bazalgette de Charneve amongst the nobles nominated to the Estates General convened in 1789.

Joseph's grandfather, Jean-Louis, left France in around 1770 for the Americas and ended up a landowner in Jamaica. He arrived in England in 1775, and on August 14, 1779, he married a Katherine Metivier. Jean-Louis established himself as a merchant on Little Grosvenor Street and by 1789 had built up a considerable fortune.

Records indicate he was in the habit of lending money to several prominent members of English society, including a number of members of the royal household.

On October 18, 1792, Jean-Louis became a British citizen and purchased a large estate at Eastwick Park in Surrey. He had three children from his first marriage, the first of which was Joseph William Bazalgette, born in 1783. This boy would become the father of the engineer who is the subject of this book. But before that, Joseph William would enlist in the Royal Navy. He was wounded in an engagement in March 1809 and invalided out of Navy with a pension for life. His only son, also named Joseph William, would be born on March 28, 1819, at Enfield.

The younger Bazalgette was, then, born into a family of means. His father had been lamed for life by his injury but was supported by his Navy pension. His grandfather was a man of property and title, including property overseas, and of considerable wealth. That his parents were at least comfortably off is demonstrated by his private education. By 1836, at the age of 17, Bazalgette was an articled pupil of Sir John MacNeill. To be articled meant that he was bound by a written contract to a period of apprenticeship. His mentor, Sir John MacNeill, had been a principal assistant to the great bridge and roadbuilder Thomas Telford.

Chapter Two

Civil Engineer

"I get most credit for the Thames Embankment but it wasn't anything like such a job as the drainage."

—Joseph Bazalgette

Bazalgette was employed by Sir John McNeill as a resident engineer concerning land drainage and reclamation work in Northern Ireland until 1838 and then spent a year as a railway route surveyor. By 1842, at the age of 23, he had founded his own civil engineering consultancy firm. He established himself in offices on Great George Street. At the time, this street was renowned for its engineering offices, and the premises which Bazalgette took over had previously been occupied by both of the famous Stephensons.

In 1845, while engaged in railway surveying work, Bazalgette married Maria Kough. But although his personal life seemed to be going well, his work at the railway was so intense that he suffered a nervous breakdown two years later. This period was the height of the railway mania, which had been sparked by the success of George Stephenson's first public railway line, the Liverpool-Manchester, as well as the Great Western Railway built by Isambard Kingdom Brunel. The entire country was being criss-crossed with railway lines, and good engineers were heavily in demand to survey the proposed routes. Bazalgette undertook this work as the head of a team of engineers who worked across the United Kingdom; he conducted a variety of transport-related engineering works, including ship canals as well as railways.

For such a young man to be so in demand is a testament to Bazalgette's success and the ability he had as an engineer. In his applications for jobs, he was able to quote as references the likes of Robert Stephenson (son of George Stephenson, co-designer of the famous Rocket locomotive and builder of the London to Birmingham railway), Sir William Cubitt (engineer for the Great Northern Railway), and last, but most definitely not least, Isambard Kingdom Brunel himself.

This early work was to prove essential in Bazalgette's skills and experience. At the time, any proposed railway line required parliamentary approval, so an engineer had to be capable of navigating the corridors of power in Westminster as well as carrying out the practical work of surveying. Political connections as well professional were essential.

On February 17, 1846, Bazalgette became a full member of the Institute of Civil Engineers. The *Proceedings of the Institute of Civil Engineers* document over one hundred contributions by Bazalgette either as his own papers or a contributor to discussions on others. Of his own work, there was a paper on land reclamation from the sea, drawing on his experience from Northern Ireland.

His contributions to the work of others include sewage treatment processes, comments on papers to do with the water supply to fountains in Trafalgar Square, the use of mechanisms for dredging, and the problems entailed in the construction of a tunnel from Calais to Dover.

Just three days after being elected to the Institute, Bazalgette became a father for the first time. His son, Joseph William, was born on February 20, 1846. Joseph William would be followed by ten other children over the next fifteen years: Charles Norman (1847), Edward (1848), Theresa Philo (1850), Caroline (1852), Maria (1854), Henry (1855), Willoughby (1857), Maria Louise (1859), Anna Constance (1859), and Evelyn (1861). By 1851, Bazalgette and his family moved from their residence at 17 Hamilton Terrace, St John's Wood in the north west of London to Morden in the south-west of central London.

The prosperity of the Bazalgette family aided Joseph's career as an engineer; his grandfather would certainly have been a well-respected member of county society due to his wealth, propertied and titled status, and his aristocratic background. The political connections which Bazalgette possessed would prove useful in the next phase of his career.

Chapter Three
The Big Stink

"The appearance and the smell of the water forced themselves at once upon my attention. The whole of the river was an opaque, pale brown fluid. . . . The smell was very bad . . . If we neglect this subject, we cannot expect to do so with impunity, nor ought we to be surprised if, ere many years are over, a hot season gives us sad proof of the folly of our carelessness."

—Michael Faraday

Bazalgette's expertise in drainage and the transportation of water was based on his years as a pupil to Sir John MacNeill. But it was his work on developing a sewage system for London that was to cement his reputation in this area. This work involved the construction of fully enclosed brick tunnels beneath the streets of the capital to carry away sewage from homes instead of allowing it be deposited directly into the River Thames. To understand the importance of this work, it is first necessary to look at the water and drainage systems in place in London before Bazalgette.

For centuries the inhabitants of London had taken little pride in the quality of their water supply and the ingenuity of the mechanisms by which it was made available . This began with a system of clay pipes laid by the Romans to carry water from the Walbrook to various public baths and amenities. By the Middle Ages, Londoners obtained their water from the Thames, its many tributaries, and various wells around the city.

From the thirteenth century onwards, civil engineering projects led to the construction of pipe systems made of a variety of materials, ranging from clay to hollowed out tree trunks. In 1237, Gilbert de Sandford granted to the city the springs on his lands at Mary le Bourne. This water was piped in lead pipes to a conduit in Cheapside where it was available for householders to draw on. A century later in 1439, the abbot of Westminster granted London the right to build wells in his manor of Paddington. Then in 1582, Peter Morice leased the first arch of London Bridge from the city for the purposes of constructing a water wheel. For the next 240 years, this wheel scooped water out of the river to be pumped back into London's water supply.

As the population of London expanded, so did the need for water. From the first medieval civil engineering projects there came a succession of projects to increase the water supply of the capital. But to this point, there was no examination of the cleanliness of the water. In fact, there was no real understanding of the link between dirty water and disease without microbiology to identify disease-causing bacteria in the water. Thus London's water projects continued to revolve around bringing more water sources into the reach of the city.

In 1613, Thomas Middleton, a Member of Parliament, began construction of the New River, which diverted a spring in Hertfordshire a distance of 40 miles. The New River remains a source of London's water to this day.

Beginning in the sixteenth century and continuing with the expansion of London's population, many of the tributaries to the Thames were covered over and became streets; underneath the streets, the streams continued to flow.

In 1532, the Bill of Sewers had led to the creation of Commissioners of Sewers whose job it was to check the adequacy of drainage systems in their respective areas. This included ensuring that cesspools were being used for the collection of human waste and that this was not being emptied into the Thames' tributaries. Despite this prohibition, the cesspools themselves had contributed to pollution problems. They were not designed to be watertight and allowed much of the liquid waste to seep away into soil and sand. Ultimately, the waste found its way into the water table and the river.

This pollution became an increasing problem as the Thames came to be the primary source of water for Londoners. From 1723 onwards, numerous companies were established to draw water out of the river and pump it back into the city for consumption. There was an atmosphere of complacency concerning the adequacy of London's drinking water. In 1828, a Royal Commission into the matter employed the celebrated engineer Thomas Telford to look at a solution. He recommended bringing in fresh, uncontaminated water from outside London.

This did not address the actual problem of contamination, and his recommendations were not acted upon anyway due to cost.

One of the witnesses giving evidence before this Commission was one Dr. Pearson. In his view, the contents of Thames water were as harmless as the minerals imbuing pure spring water. Dr. Pearson expressed the opinion that there were few springs in the country with water so pure as Thames water. And in 1844, a professor of chemistry, Professor Booth, wrote in the journal *The Builder* that the water of the River Thames was the main source of the "salubrity of the metropolis." In his opinion, the water of the Thames was not only an adequate source of drinking water, but it would also contribute to health.

There were those who believed differently, though their understanding of the true dangers of drinking contaminated water was flawed. Until as late as the early twentieth century, it was generally accepted that diseases such as cholera were miasmic. In other words, the infection was spread through the air, in particular the foul fumes exuded from contaminated water. London began to experience cholera epidemics from 1831 onwards. One physician, John Snow, noticed that deaths were greater in areas supplied by certain water companies and posited that the disease was waterborne, but his theories were largely ignored. Despite the erroneous views on how dirty water spread disease, however, the remedies would still prove to be effective.

In 1844, the Building Act required all buildings and cesspools to be connected to a sewer. Because of the fear of miasma from these sewers, the decision was made to flush them through on a regular basis to prevent the build-up of gases. This had the effect of increasing the levels of raw sewage being emptied into the Thames. In 1848, the Metropolitan Commission of Sewers was created at the urging of Edwin Chadwick, a social reformer of some influence. By the mid-nineteenth century, water closets were increasingly popular with Londoners, and the emergence of this innovation had increased the amount of waste which the antiquated sewer system was forced to deal with.

Additionally, the maintenance of that sewer system was overseen by seven authorities covering the whole of London, who had been in existence since the reign of Henry VIII. There was little co-operation or sharing of ideas between these bodies, and the result was differences in workmanship standards. While one authority improved its systems, they caused an increase of pressure on their neighbor's. The formation of a single, unitary authority to deal with the drainage problems of London would solve that problem. And in August 1849, Joseph Bazalgette was appointed to the position of assistant surveyor with the Metropolitan Sewers Commission (MSC).

Chapter Four

Metropolitan Commissions for Sewers

"A certain flush with every pull!"

—Marketing tagline for Thomas Crapper's water closets

The first Metropolitan Commission for Sewers number one priority was ensuring that every dwelling was in accordance with the 1844 Buildings Act, requiring a dwelling to be equipped with a connection to the nearest sewer, as well as an ash pit and a WC. The policy pursued by the Commission was one of "no filth in the sewers, all in the river."

To modern ears this would seem a ludicrous policy, but in an age where it was not understood that diseases like cholera were waterborne, it made sense. Removing waste from tidal sewers, which would overflow into homes at high tide, would remove the miasma which was believed to cause the disease. If the wastewater was in the river, the odor would not be in the home or the streets. So, from September 1848 to February 1849, some 80,000 cubic yards of sewage was flushed from sewers into the river.

Bazalgette's involvement arose with the second Commission, which took office on January 1, 1849. The Commission included Cuthbert Johnson, a manure expert, and was to look at converting sewage into fertilizer for commercial use. The Commission's consulting engineer, Henry Austin, drew up a plan to achieve this by gathering the sewage into four reservoirs from which it could then be pumped out for agricultural use. The Commission's chief surveyor, John Phillips, came up with a rival plan which involved the construction of intercepting sewer tunnels that would carry sewage away to Plumstead Marshes. Both men claimed their schemes would be highly profitable and would easily recoup the construction costs.

The Commission became divided into two camps, each backing one of the schemes. An agreement could not be reached, and so on August 16, 1849, a general invitation was issued to engineers to submit their own schemes. The second Commission was dissolved when agreement could still not be reached, and on October 8, 1849, a third Commission was formed. This became known as the Engineer's Commission because of the presence among its members of prominent engineers such as Robert Stephenson. A sub-committee was created to review the submissions which had been received by the second Commission, and Joseph Bazalgette was given the task of reviewing these submissions.

Bazalgette grouped the submissions into categories and then presented his report to the Committee which announced on March 8, 1850 that none of the proposals was entirely satisfactory. Though Bazalgette had experience in drainage engineering, he must have gained valuable intelligence on the particular problem of draining London's sewage by his task of reviewing these proposals. He was given an insight into what the political elite would consider as a solution as well as the financial limitations in place at the time. He would also have been able to observe what particular theories were favored by influential members of the Commission. All of this would have served him well when his time came to propose a solution of his own.

For the moment, however, the Commission fell back on the services of its chief engineer, Frank Forster, a former railway engineer and colleague of Robert Stephenson. On August 1, 1850, Forster submitted plans for a drainage system on the south side of the river involving an intercepting sewer which would discharge into the river. On January 31, 1851, a proposal was put forward for the north side. His scheme omitted a 16-square-mile area of Fulham and Hammersmith which posed problems because it was low-lying. These problems would be solved in Bazalgette's proposal. The work would run significantly over budget and lead to the resignation of the third Commission. Forster then died during the term of the fourth Commission owing to the stress of the job, and Bazalgette was appointed as his successor.

At this time, Bazalgette was not concerned with preventing sewage and other effluent from reaching the river, but rather with ensuring that all properties were connected to an effective sewage system. A fifth

Commission, to which he was the chief engineer, was formed after October 1852 and considered a private Bill proposed by the Great London Drainage Company. The company wanted to construct two intercepting sewers which would divert sewage for agricultural use.

As chief engineer to the fifth Commission, Bazalgette began working with William Haywood, engineer to the City of London. They reviewed Forster's plans and modified them. These modified plans were subsequently approved by Robert Stephenson and William Cubitt, who were consulting engineers to the Commission.

But unfortunately, the fifth Commission lacked the funds to begin construction of the sewer system; they would not be able to purchase lands where pumping stations would be built or to compensate landowners for allowing the sewer to run through their property. Appeals to Parliament were to no avail, and the fifth Commission resigned in 1854. It would be briefly replaced by a sixth Commission before the passage of the Metropolis Management Act on August 17, 1855, which provided for the foundation of the Metropolitan Board of Works that took over from the commissions.

Chapter Five

Metropolitan Board of Works

"It was a notorious fact that honourary Gentlemen sitting in the Committee rooms and in the library were utterly unable to remain there in consequences of the stench which arose from the river."

—Hansard, June 7, 1858

The Metropolitan Board of Works was the first central government for the City of London. It was granted power to carry out construction projects including roads, bridges, parks, and sewers. On January 1, 1856, Joseph Bazalgette was formally asked to be chief engineer to the new Board of Works, effectively continuing the role he had held under the ill-fated commissions.

His appointment was confirmed on January 25, 1856, after being supported by Robert Stephenson, Isambard Kingdom Brunel, and William Cubitt. Bazalgette's reputation was clearly established if such illustrious men were willing to endorse him, particularly for what must have been recognized as a crucial job for the City of London.

On February 18, 1856, the Board passed a resolution requiring Bazalgette to report to them the plans necessary to prevent the sewage from reaching the Thames. This was to be the first priority.

Bazalgette's immediate superior in the Board of Works was John Thwaites, a former draper who had risen in local politics to chair the sixth and final Metropolitan Commission. Thwaites had been publicly critical of Bazalgette following an incident in which Bazalgette had been required to establish the efficacy of brick or earthenware for the construction of sewage pipes. Bazalgette found in favor of brick, but his methods in surveying the sewers of London and five other towns were found to be wanting in diligence. Thwaites believed that Bazalgette had not carried out an objective review and had merely found in favor of his employers. It is a good indication of the character of Joseph Bazalgette that he was able to put these differences aside to work under Thwaites at the MBW and even appoint John Grant—another of his critics—to be his deputy.

Following the issuing of instructions to him by the Board, Bazalgette responded quickly with his plans. This was, after all, a problem which he was well acquainted with after his numerous years working for the commissions. On April 4, 1856, he submitted his plans for the sewage system south of the river, followed by the north on May 23. His presentation was humble, making reference to the work undertaken by others, such as Forster and the engineers responding to the open contest of the third Commission in 1850:

"Almost every suggestion which can be made upon the subject has been so often repeated in some shape or other that it would be difficult to detect which were the first authors of the various schemes propounded. Having had the advantage of access to all, I cannot pretend to much originality; my endeavor has been practically to apply suggestions, originating in a large measure with others, to the peculiar wants and features of different districts, with which my position has made me familiar."

These words are here quoted as a demonstration of the diffident personality of the man. Bazalgette's humility is in marked contrast to other prominent engineers of the nineteenth century. One of the articled apprentices who would serve under him at the Metropolitan Board of Works described him as having meticulous attention to detail; he described the praise he received for a drawing he had completed, but which Bazalgette then critiqued because his handwriting was untidy.

Bazalgette was small in height and suffered from asthma. He was described as having seemingly limitless patience and persistence. This can be seen in the way he was able to handle the demanding commission given to him by the Board of Works, one which had brought about the early death of Frank Forster.

Chapter Six

Bazalgette's Plan

"The most extensive and wonderful work of modern times."

—*The Observer*, 1861

The system devised by Bazalgette was for the land north of the river to be drained by three intercepting sewers, while two would be provided for south of the river. North of the river, low-level sewers would be pumped up to the level of the high-level sewers with the combined flow guided into the Thames at a point west of the River Roding, near Barking. On the south side, a similar operation but in reverse would be established; high-level sewers would empty to low level and then discharge into the river at Crossness, further eastward along the river than the northern outflow.

These outflows would be collected in balancing tanks at Beckton and Crossness before being dumped at high tide into the river. In total, Bazalgette's plan would call for 82 miles of main sewers, each a completely enclosed underground tunnel made of brick. It would also require 1,100 miles of street sewers; these would be tributaries to the main sewers and would carry the effluent and rainwater from street level and homes.

On June 3, 1856, the plan was submitted to the first commissioner of the Board of Works, Benjamin Hall. Hall's role was to oversee the work of the MBW, providing parliamentary oversight to the Board's projects. He submitted the plans to an independent consultant, Captain Burstall, who ruled that the plans were in breach of the Metropolis Act 1855, which had led to the creation of the Board of Works. The Act stated that the Board of Works should make sewers to prevent all wastewater from flowing into the Thames in or near the metropolis. Burstall argued that the outflow sites were within the metropolitan boundary and therefore in breach of the Act.

A stalemate was reached as Bazalgette and Thwaites negotiated with Hall over modifications to the plans. For Bazalgette this would have been a difficult juggling act. If the sewage was not sufficiently far from the Houses of Parliament, then Members of Parliament affected by the stench would be in uproar, putting his career in jeopardy. On the other hand, the more expensive the project became, the more the local councils of various London districts would have to pay for the construction and upkeep. Either way, Bazalgette would have known that his reputation was at stake. In fact, the pressure from Parliament was already being exerted through Benjamin Hall because of the stench of the river where it flowed past the Palace of Westminster.

The summer of 1858 was particularly dry and hot, gaining infamy as the year of the "Big Stink." It was now that politicians in Westminster became fully aware of the need to act on the subject of sewage in the Thames. The problem was quite literally under their noses and impossible to ignore.

On July 15, 1858, a bill was proposed by Benjamin Disraeli called the Metropolis Local Management Amendment Act. This was meant to amend the bill passed in 1855, which was hampering the MBW's attempts to implement Bazalgette's plans. The key amendments removed the sticky wording on the subject of disposal of sewage "in or near the Metropolis." Instead, the Board of Works was called upon to ensure that sewage was disposed away from the metropolis "as far as may be practicable."

The amended bill also removed Parliament's right of veto against any Board project and enabled the Board to raise money to fund their works, underwritten by the Treasury. As a result of the 1858 Metropolis Local Management Amendment Act, the MBW now had the funds and the authority to go ahead. Joseph Bazalgette could finally begin to build.

Bazalgette's design called for three main intercepting sewers north of the river. These would be high level, middle level, and low level to allow for the terrain they had to cross. The high-level sewer covered nine miles from Hampstead Heath in northwest London to Stratford in the northeast corner of the city. It lay between 20 and 26 feet beneath the surface and would be built beneath such obstacles as the New River, the Great Northern Railway, and the Grand Union Canal.

At Stratford, the middle and high-level main sewers met. The low-level sewer followed the river and involved the construction of the now famous embankments. The construction of the eventual outflow of the sewers in the far eastern end of the city would require temporary cement works and rail lines to be built to keep the construction supplied. It would also require roads to be raised to allow for the sewers pass beneath them and the construction of large embankments to carry the sewers across low-lying marshy ground.

In the western part of the city, around Hammersmith, there was a particular problem posed by the low level of the ground which meant that gravity could not be relied upon to allow the sewers to discharge into the main system. It is illustrative of attitudes of the time that Bazalgette's first solution was to collect the sewage in this area into a reservoir, deodorize it, and then release it into the river. He reasoned that the population of the area was relatively small and so could not have a large impact on the amount of effluent entering the river.

It is important to note that though the goal of the work was to clean up the Thames, it was not driven by any environmental concerns that we would recognize today. To empty untreated sewage into the river was not seen as unacceptable. The goal was simply to reduce the "Big Stink," which was believed to cause diseases like cholera. Thus, to Bazalgette and the Board of Works, it was considered acceptable to release sewage into the river where it would be drawn into drinking water provided the smell was removed.

But the plan was halted by protests in the area by the Fulham medical officer, Dr. Burge. After the Society of Medical Officers and Public Health sent a deputation to the Board of Works in January 1863, Bazalgette was forced to change his plans. Eventually, a pumping station would serve to elevate the sewage into the low-level sewer.

South of the river would be similar to the scheme in place for the north, though covering a much smaller population. The combined length of the sewer was 12 miles and ended in the outfall at Crossness. Here four engines would lift the sewage 21 feet into a reservoir, from where it would enter the river at high tide. These engines were the largest of their kind and survive to this day. The same is also true for the brick tunnels which formed the main sewers. Bazalgette carefully calculated the number of people in each area of London and how much sewage those people could produce. Then he doubled that figure and based the diameter of the tunnels on that exaggerated figure. In this way, he allowed for the dramatic expansion of population that London would see in the next hundred years.

Bazalgette also overestimated the amount of water the system would have to cope with, in particular the lifting stations. He did this by examining the water supply to the current population, making his estimates for population expansion, and then increasing both. He also increased the amount of rainfall which the system would be able to cope with. This was tested on July 26, 1867, when an unprecedented amount of rain fell overnight, more than twice the maximum which the lifting engines had been designed to move. Despite the heavy rain, the system worked. It was a remarkable piece of foresight that would ensure that his drainage system would not need to be overhauled or expanded in any major way in the decades to come.

In total there would be 82 miles of main sewer running parallel to the Thames to the outflows at Barking and Crossness. There would be an additional 1,100 miles of subsidiary tunnels. Construction was put out to tender and contractors were hired to undertake the work. Bazalgette was a perfectionist and seems to have been unable to allow any aspect of the project, no matter how small, to escape his notice. For example, he chose a particular kind of brick for the sewer tunnels known as Staffordshire Blues which were particularly hardy. This was to withstand the scouring effect of water falling through the system from high to low level.

Bazalgette's insistence on the use of Portland cement was illustrative of his self-belief and unwillingness to be swayed by the views of others. It had been patented in 1824 by a Yorkshire bricklayer named Joseph Aspdin. The new cement was regarded as impressive in its strength but was generally regarded as being unreliable. This was because it was sensitive to a very narrow range of conditions in its production process. Deviations from the correct quantities of materials or temperatures would have a significant effect on the eventual strength of the product.

The consensus view among builders and engineers at the time was that the more traditional Roman cement was the appropriate material to use on large-scale projects. This view was reinforced by endorsements from the leading builders of the age such as Brunel, who used Roman cement on his Thames Tunnel, and Robert Stephenson, who used it in railway buildings.

But there was one property of Portland cement that made it the most suitable for Bazalgette's purposes; it was known to be resistant to water and, in fact, to gain strength when continually exposed to water. For a project in which the construction would be constantly exposed to water, or even submerged, this property was an attractive one. Bazalgette decided, against conventional wisdom, that Portland cement would be used. It was a bold decision as it would be the first time the material had been used in any large-scale public project.

It was not just in his decision to use a new material that Bazalgette broke new ground. Portland cement had rightly earned its reputation for unreliability because of the relative lack of quality testing done by the manufacturers. Bazalgette instructed his assistants to carry out rigorous testing of the material to ascertain its true strength. He wrote detailed instructions as to exactly how the material should be treated, stored, and tested, including precisely how those tests should be carried out. These tests were presented to the Institute of Civil Engineers by his assistant John Grant in December 1865 and caused four straight days of debate on the subject. Despite being the deviser of the tests and the man whose reputation hung on the use of this previously untested material, Bazalgette appears to have been unconcerned that it was his assistant who presented the findings to the Institute, further demonstration of his personality.

Having tested the strength of the cement, there remained the question of the rudimentary quality control in place where the cement was being manufactured. In order to mitigate the risk of using a weak batch, he imposed his own rigorous quality controls on site. Every single batch of cement was tested, with the samples tested to destruction. His contractors were ordered to reject the entire batch if the sample failed the test. Such rigor resulted in the suppliers soon implementing their own quality control standards, to avoid losing contracts to Bazalgette's eye for detail.

The first stage of the project was completed by April 1865 and comprised the southern system. The northern system would be completed three years later, ten years after the first works began. Ten years after that, in 1875, the last area of London was finally connected to the main sewer system.

Chapter Seven

The Embankments

"For the principal engineer, of course, it will be a monument of enduring fame, second to none of the great achievements that have marked the Victorian age."

—*The Times*, July 1870

The embankments of London are now a well-known landmark and a name which even those who have never visited London would probably recognize as belonging to the city. The embankments, which were constructed on the north (Chelsea and Victoria) and south (Albert) of the river, were designed and built by Joseph Bazalgette and were a crucial part of his grand drainage plan.

North of the river, the main thoroughfare was the Strand, which connected the financial center of the City of London to the governmental center of Westminster. This was an exceptionally busy street during the day and was frequently jammed with vehicles. Despite this, the low-level main sewer needed to run along the path of the Strand, following the course of the river. It was unthinkable to dig up this busy thoroughfare in order to lay the sewers as the disruption would have been huge. The solution was to reclaim land from the river to form three embankments, which would provide new alternative routes, thus easing congestion, and provide a place to house the main sewers as well as other underground systems such as the underground rail and gas line.

The task of building the embankments was as significant an engineering project as the sewer project which had brought the need for the embankments into being. In all, 52 acres of land would need to be reclaimed from the river. The Victoria Embankment began construction in 1865, but it was the Albert Embankment, south of the river, that would be completed first. Its purpose was not to incorporate a main sewer (as the northern embankments were intended to do) but instead to protect the low-lying district of Lambeth from flooding. The Albert Embankment began construction in July 1866 and was completed in November 1869. Upon its completion, one of London's most notable buildings would end up being built on it, namely St. Thomas' Hospital which was relocated from Southwark to its new home on the Albert Embankment.

But it was the Victoria Embankment that attracted the greatest attention. This would be the new thoroughfare connecting Westminster to the city, and it was also intended to house the main low-level sewer. Without reclaiming land to house the main sewer, the only other alternative would be run the sewer under the Strand, Fleet Street, and Ludgate Hill, all of which were notorious for their congestion. The embankment would also serve to provide a new thoroughfare connecting the financial center to Westminster and provide Londoners a welcome green space in the busiest part of the capital. It replaced a foreshore of dilapidated houses and warehouses and sewage-laden mudbanks. Another important role it played was housing the underground railway line from Blackfriars to Westminster underground stations. This proved important in the eventual construction of the Circle Line which ran around the City of London and Westminster.

It was clear from the outset that Bazalgette did not intend the Victoria Embankment to be in any way utilitarian in the way that a seawall might be. He commissioned for artists' impressions of his own designs, and these were widely circulated, generating much interest in the project among the public and press. It incorporated a concave retaining wall against the river made from 650,000 cubic feet of granite. It was decorated with bronze mooring rings which had been cast in the shape of lion heads. These decorations were lit with cast iron lamps which were themselves shaped like dolphins.

The Victoria Embankment would become a wide boulevard lined with trees and including open green spaces in the form of the Embankment Gardens. It's over a mile long, and as well as housing the main low-level sewer, it would also cover gas and water mains while incorporating mooring points for river steamers. Later it would carry electricity cables and become the first street in London to be electrified. It solved multiple problems while being flexible enough in its design to allow for future developments.

The embankment was opened on July 13, 1870 with great pomp and ceremony. The inauguration was opened by the prince of Wales along with five other members of the royal family. It was also attended by 24 ambassadors, almost all members of Houses of Parliament, and 10,000 members of the public. Few civil engineering projects, even those of Telford, Brunel, and Stephenson, attracted England's elite in such numbers.

While Bazalgette's work in the design and construction of the new sewer system was undoubtedly vital to the survival and growth of London and subject to press attention, it was hardly the kind of project that would cement his name in the imaginations of the average man in the street. But the Victoria Embankment was different, and Bazalgette would have achieved the status of household name when it was opened. It was a concrete and very visible example of how Bazalgette's work was improving the city and the lives of Londoners.

Initially, however, there was a threat from the highest levels of government that would have transformed the Victoria Embankment completely. William Gladstone, the prime minister, wanted to seize the newly reclaimed land for the Crown and then lease out space on the embankment for the construction of offices and other commercial properties. With this revenue, he hoped to abolish the income tax which had been imposed on British subjects for the first time during the Napoleonic War. Had Gladstone been successful in his ambitions, this area of London would look radically different. It would have become choked with buildings, and Londoners would have been denied a rare open space and wide boulevard along the river.

Gladstone persisted with his plan against stiff public opposition orchestrated in the press by former newsagent and Member of Parliament W.H. Smith. Bazalgette was also, understandably, opposed to Gladstone's proposition as it would have wiped out his design work for the embankment. As has already been mentioned, the designs he drew up and the care taken in the illustrations of those designs demonstrate that this was not to be a simple engineering project but one with high aesthetic values as well.

When Bazalgette attended a public meeting at St. James's Hall in Piccadilly, which was attended by several hundred members of the public, he received cheers while the prime minister was booed. To the public's relief, Gladstone's plan was eventually dropped. So, while the London public may not have recognized the name Bazalgette based on his largely invisible drainage work, they knew him from the famous Victoria Embankment.

In July 1871, work began on the Chelsea Embankment. This was the second of the two embankments constructed on the north side of the river. It was opened on July 9, 1874, and later in July, Joseph Bazalgette was knighted.

Chapter Eight

Transport for London

"Evidence of strong prejudice in favor of all street improvements within or leading directly towards, the City and an equally strong objection to any which do not appear to lead the traffic direct into the City."

—Joseph Bazalgette

In 1856, a report was published by a Parliamentary Select Committee on the subject of population increase in London. It noted that in the preceding 40 years the population had more than doubled, and as a result, traffic on London's streets had also increased significantly. This was beginning to cause congestion problems, particularly at London's established train stations. It was estimated that eleven million passengers were using London Bridge station annually with eight million to Fenchurch and three million to Waterloo. A number of solutions were considered to solve the problem of this increase in passengers that the existing infrastructure could not cope with.

The Committee also decided that new through routes and a metropolitan railway connecting London's disparate hub stations should be constructed and tolls removed on all London bridges. It also decreed that this work should fall to the Metropolitan Board of Works. These responsibilities, along with the issue of the sewer system, fell to Joseph Bazalgette as the MWB's chief engineer. For the Board report of 1858-1859, he prepared a list of proposals detailing how these responsibilities might be achieved.

The work to open new thoroughfares in London was delayed from this initial report due to political wranglings. Every proposal had to be approved by the home secretary, which caused delays. Any proposal to demolish slum dwellings was refused until the residents had been rehoused, which caused problems due to the lack of places to rehouse them into. With the majority of their borrowing and investment returns funding the drainage project, the Board of Works had little or no funds left to purchase properties they needed to remove.

Then there was the problem of vested interests. The areas where new thoroughfares were being proposed were relatively small. While the areas that would benefit were willing to support Bazalgette's plans, he found opposition arising in areas which were not in any way affected. The problem was that the Board itself comprised representatives from various local political areas of London. Each of these so-called vestries (the equivalent of the local government authorities which modern London is divided into) had their own interests at the forefront and looked with chagrin at anything that would cost ratepayers in their areas money.

In addition, the Corporation of the City of London (the financial district) had its own vested interests, which consisted of getting as many people and tradesmen into London as they could and being in opposition to anything that did not achieve this goal. Bazalgette showed his dismay at the situation, commenting on the "strong prejudices in favor of all street improvements within, or leading directly towards the City, and an equally strong objection to any which do not appear to lead the traffic directly into the City."

While construction on the Victoria Embankment was underway, it became clear to Bazalgette that a through road connecting the western end of the embankment with Trafalgar Square and the Strand would be important. The problem was that Northumberland House, home to the Percy family, dukes of Northumberland, lay directly in the way. Eventually, the house was purchased from the family, and Northumberland Avenue was completed in 1876. The street was given a wide carriage to allow for tall buildings to either side, as the cost of construction was intended to be recouped by leasing the buildings facing onto the street to commercial enterprises like hotels. This proved to be especially popular with Americans due to its proximity to Whitehall and mainline stations.

Following the opening of Northumberland Avenue, Bazalgette and architect George Vulliamy went to work on Shaftesbury Avenue. This would be a north to south artery through the districts of St Giles and Soho. The building of Shaftesbury Avenue would also serve to clear slums in these overcrowded areas. Charing Cross Road and Garrick Street both served the same purpose, demolishing slums and creating new thoroughfares that would ease congestion on existing routes.

During the construction of Charis Cross Road, Bazalgette needed to demolish the notorious slums of St Giles. These had been declared unfit for human habitation. But before they could be demolished, the Board of Works had to check the ownership of the properties. The Home Secretary then had to appoint an adjudicator and provide compensation based on the going rate for the buildings, even if they were condemned. Then there was the problem of rehousing the people who had been living there.

The red tape was considerable, and it would be six years before Bazalgette could finally go to work on Charing Cross Road. His final obstacle was the historic church of St Martin-in-the-fields. The route for Charing Cross Road ran close to the front entrance of the church, and Bazalgette appears to have decided that it would be acceptable for his new road to cut through the steps that decorate the classical portico for which the building is renowned. He further proposed to brick up the portico itself. This plan was changed following the understandable outcry from the church's parishioners. Bazalgette adjusted the route of the new road to spare the church.

The problem posed by the need to rehouse the inhabitants of slum dwellings was not limited to Charing Cross. Responsibility for the elimination of the slums had been given to the Board of Works in the 1855 Artisans' and Labourers' Dwellings Improvements Act. The Earl of

Shaftesbury, a noted philanthropist, had given evidence to a Parliamentary Select Committee which highlighted the scale of the problem. In his testimony, he described a visit to a notorious area of Holborn known as Frying Pan Alley. There he encountered a woman sitting next to a wide hole in her floor. She explained to him how either she or her husband had to stay awake during the night because of the problem with rats coming up from the sewers.

Meanwhile in Bermondsey, which was a low-lying area of the city, homes had been built onto a bed of sewage known as Jacob's Island. Residents of Jacob's Island drew washing and drinking water from the surrounding area, which was permanently befouled. Bazalgette's intercepting sewer served to eliminate the problem of sewage, cleaning up the water in the area and leaving what had been a festering swamp as dry land. Board works to demolish slum dwellings then enabled the previously condemned homes to be replaced with sanitary ones.

In this work, Bazalgette played another pivotal role in replacing the London of antiquity with the city which would be more recognizable to Londoners today. As with his sewer system and the Embankments, it is a testament to his skill as a surveyor, planner, and engineer that the routes which he proposed—Northumberland Avenue, Shaftesbury Avenue, Charing Cross Road, and Garrick Street—are pivotal arteries running through London to this day. Northumberland Avenue even appears on the Monopoly board. A less skilled planner might have found their changes rendered obsolete, requiring further work and outlay. But Bazalgette's plans all seem to have been drawn up with a shrewd eye for what would be needed for decades to come.

In total, Joseph Bazalgette was responsible for 42 major improvements to London's road system. In the process of making these improvements, he was responsible for demolishing 7,403 slum tenements and rehousing 38,231 people. Without his work, many would have died from the unsanitary conditions in which they were forced to live.

Chapter Nine

Bridges Across the Thames

"Londoners who can remember the state of London and of the Thames about thirty-five years ago, before those vast undertakings of the Metropolitan Board of Works, the system of main drainage and the magnificent Thames Embankment, which have contributed some much to sanitary improvement and to the convenience and stateliness of this immense city, will regret the death of the able official chief engineer, Sir Joseph Bazalgette."

—*Illustrated London News*, March 1891

The final area of responsibility handed to the Board of Works by the Select Committee on Metropolitan Communications was to relieve London of the burden of toll bridges. In the 1850s, the only toll-free crossings of the Thames were London Bridge, Blackfriars Bridge, and Westminster Bridge. In 1866, Southwark Bridge was added to this list when it was purchased from private hands. All other bridges across the Thames had been paid for privately and were intended to make profit for investors.

The Select Committee considered this unfair to the working classes, particularly as the poorest parts of London were located south of the river, while many of the jobs were north. It was calculated that a significant proportion of workers' wages were spent on tolls every year. The average toll was a halfpenny for a pedestrian and threepence for a carriage. It was estimated that a laborer living south of the river and working north would pay, on average, 24 shillings a year from an annual wage of 40 to 50 pounds.

The Board of Works was charged with freeing these bridges from private hands and thus making them toll-free. The problem that emerged was that some crossings, such as Waterloo Bridge, had not proved profitable and had been allowed to deteriorate. Similar situations were evidenced elsewhere, such as the Albert Bridge (connecting Chelsea in the north to Battersea in the south) and the Hammersmith Bridge. There was also the problem of degeneration as bridges had been designed and built for the population and traffic of an earlier age. In Hammersmith, the original bridge design proved woefully inadequate to cope with the volume of traffic a modern Thames bridge would be required to deal with.

Bazalgette was forced to redesign and rebuild the Albert Bridge between 1884 and 1877 as its original design (only ten years old) was proving structurally unsound. He added in design elements of a suspension bridge, and these changes were sufficient to maintain the bridge until the 1970s when further enhancements were deemed necessary. He also replaced wooden bridges at Battersea and Putney which proved to be beyond repair.

At Battersea, the original wooden bridge had been built in 1772 and was completely demolished. Bazalgette's design replaced it, a five-arch structure. At Putney, a pontoon bridge had first been built during the civil war in 1642 to aid Parliamentary troops in crossing the river. In 1729, a wooden bridge was built on the site which survived until the 1880s. This structure proved too narrow, though, to cope with the increased traffic resulting from the end of the tolls. Bazalgette constructed a granite bridge to replace the old one. He also widened the road approaching Putney Bridge to accommodate the increase in traffic. All of Bazalgette's bridges survive to this day.

Between London Bridge and Putney, there were now 14 toll-free bridge available, but this still left around a third of Londoners outside of this area (east of London Bridge) with no means of getting across. To solve this problem, a variety of solutions was put forward by Bazalgette, all except one being instituted and, in keeping with his other works, remaining in place to this day. To facilitate crossing the river in the east end of London he proposed a free ferry service at Woolwich and another at Greenwich, a tunnel at Blackwall and another at Rotherhithe, and a bridge where Tower Bridge now stands.

For the Blackwall Tunnel, he proposed three bores to separate vehicular traffic, horse-drawn traffic, and pedestrians. The work was commissioned by the Board of Works in 1887, and Bazalgette estimated it would take seven years to complete. His involvement in the project ended in 1889 when the Board of Works was abolished and replaced by the London County Council. Bazalgette retired at this point, and the project was completed by Sir Alexander Binnie and Ernest William Moir. Binnie and Moir's tunnel consisted of only one bore for all traffic. This served for around 40 years before it had to be expanded to cope with additional traffic volumes. Bazalgette's design with its three tunnels would have accounted for this and would probably have served for longer.

Finally, in addition to the bridges, roads, embankments, and sewer systems that he built, Sir Joseph Bazalgette had responsibility for the maintenance and design of a great many parks throughout London. Today, green urban spaces are recognized as important for the health of the environment as well as fulfilling a strong psychological need for city dwellers. In the Victorian era, it was regarded as an opportunity to be given a breath of fresh air. The fresh air was viewed as important because of the miasmatic theory of disease spread. Even the legendary "Lady of the Lamp" Florence Nightingale believed that it was unpleasant odors arising from contaminated water that were the true vectors of diseases like cholera.

The Board of Works began to assume responsibility for maintenance of parks across the city. Whenever a new park was acquired, it fell to Bazalgette and his team of engineers to survey and assess the new acquisition. In some cases, there was a lot of drainage and landscaping required to bring the land up to a standard that allowed use by the public. In Southwark, almost 100,000 pounds was spent on landscaping and clearing of the land during the year 1869 alone. Also in 1869, a 115-acre site at Finsbury was opened after 110,000 pounds had been spent on the work.

The Greenwich ferry service was never implemented following protests from existing ferry service providers. In 1889, the newly elected London County Council took over the role which had been fulfilled by the Metropolitan Board of Works. It was the first directly elected government of London. The County Council's first chairman, Lord Roseberry, made the first act of the Council the opening of the Battersea Bridge which Bazalgette had designed. The Woolwich free crossing was also completed shortly before being handed over to the Council on January 1, 1889.

Sir Joseph Bazalgette died two years later, on Sunday, March 15, 1891 at his home, near Wimbledon. His death was marked by lengthy obituaries in national newspapers as well as in the *Proceedings of the Institution of Civil Engineers*. He had served as president of this body in 1883 to 1884 and had been a member for more than 40 years.

Conclusion

The memory of Sir Joseph Bazalgette will be forever cemented in the shape of the city in which he lived for most of his life. He cast aside slum dwellings in favor of new streets, open spaces, and parks. During his time at the Metropolitan Board of Works, he was responsible for the design of and upkeep of hundreds of parks across the city. These parks are one facet of London's international fame. That such open, green spaces can exist at the heart of one of the busiest and most crowded cities of the Western world is remarkable.

Bazalgette's work also solved problems of traffic congestion by opening new transport arteries through the heart of the city such as the Embankments, Northumberland Avenue, Shaftesbury Avenue, and Charing Cross Road. He recognized the problems of the poorer Londoners, living away from the heart of the city and in need of passage cross the river. So, not only did he cater for the two-thirds majority who lived between London Bridge and Putney by redesigning, repairing, and rebuilding the toll-free bridges, but he also catered for the remaining one-third living east of London Bridge.

Bazalgette's lifelong expertise was in the drainage of land; this is what he had learned as an apprentice to Sir John O'Neill and had worked on in his early career. He put this expertise to use in his two biggest projects: The Embankments and the main sewer construction project. These were the largest civil engineering projects of the century, both being carried out under the supervision of one man. Bazalgette insisted on strict control over his projects and could be relied upon to consider every facet—no detail was too small for his attention. And by removing the sewage from the majority of the most densely populated areas, intercepting it before it could reach the river, and carrying it away to a safe distance, Bazalgette almost eliminated the risk of cholera which had regularly plagued London to that point.

On Monday, March 16, 1891—the day after Joseph Bazalgette's passing—the *Times* published an obituary that read: "When the New Zealander comes to London, a thousand years hence, to sketch the ruins of St Paul's, the magnificent solidity and the faultless symmetry of the great granite blocks which form the wall of the Thames Embankment will still remain to testify that, in the reign of Victoria, 'jerry-building' was not quite universal. Of the great sewer that runs beneath, Londoners know, as a rule, nothing, though the Registrar-General could tell them that its existence has added twenty years to their chance of life."

Printed in Great Britain
by Amazon